To Nell o £1.50
Who will remember now
some of it.
Nancy —

Courage

1st published November, 1993.

Published by Nancy Black
Torwood, Oban PA34 4LU Scotland.

ISBN No. 0 9522830 0 X

Printed by Harlequin Press, Oban.

To the Men of the
British and Allied Merchant Navies

S.S. Samuel L. Fuller on a rock in the Sound of Mull, one of the hazards facing convoy ships sailing in coastal waters

LIST OF SHIPS AT OBAN PREPARING FOR D-DAY 1944

BRITISH		USA
Empire Moorhen	George S Wassen	Benjamin H Bristow
Empire Waterhen	West Nono	George Steers
Empire Tamar	Benjamin Contee	H G Blasdel
Empire Defiance	Matt W Ransom	William Endicott
Empire Flamingo	West Cheswald	Elmer A Sperry
Empire Tana	Victory Sword	Mahln Pitney
Panos	West Honaker	John G Whittier
Becheville	John Steele	John Grier Hibbin
Dover Hill	Lou Gehrig	
Bendoran	Joseph E Johnston	
Manchester Spinner	James A Farrell	
Mariposa	Dan Beard	
Vera Radcliffe	Horace Gray	
Innerton	Artemis Ward	
Alynbank	George Dewey	
Flowergate	Joseph Pulitzer	
Vinlake	Wilcox	
Ingman	Potter	
Elswick Park	West Grama	
Winha	Courageous	
Gold Shill	Flight Command	
Saltersgate	John A Campbell	
Prince Rupert (Tug)	David Caldwell	
Empire aid	Robert Toombs	
Forbin (French)	Joseph Storey	
Agios Spyridion (Greek)	Audacious	
Georgias P	Samuel Colt	
Lynhang (Norwegian)	George W Childs	
Sirehi	Olambala	
Njegos (Jugoslav)	James W Marshall	
Baialaide (Panamanian)	Ameriki	
Modlin (Polish)	James Iredell	
Parlaan (Dutch)	Lucius Q C Lamarr	
Belgique (Belgian)	Edward M House	

Foreword

This small book originated in an attempt to put in words a tribute to the men of our Merchant Service with whom I worked during the 1939-45 war. I hope I have succeeded.

Research was aided by *The Oban Times* files. The cover is a reproduction of one of the many posters by Fougasse which enjoined us to "keep our mouths shut". This, and most of the photographs, are reproduced by courtesy of the Imperial War Museum.

With many thanks to those who helped me put it all together.

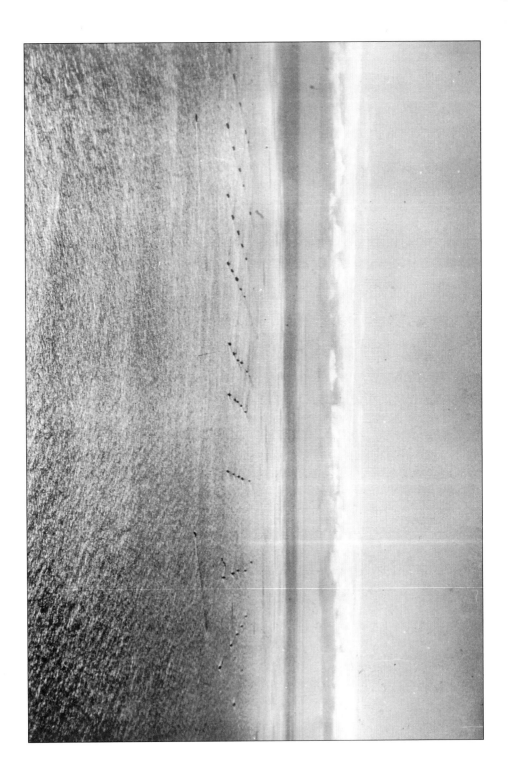

My War

by Nancy Black

With the fiftieth anniversary of the Battle of the Atlantic numerous reunions of various branches of the forces have revived interest in what actually happened in the lives of those who lived through the second World War. Later generations in Britain should stop to consider that if it were not for those who served, who decided to fight for freedom, there would be no life for them as we know it.

The British people were to have been eliminated, Europe would be run with slave labour and by this time, fifty years on, there might have been no free countries left in the world. From records found in Germany after the war the plans laid out for us all were discovered. We also learned that Oban was one of the ports pinpointed for the German invasion.

For those living in a peaceful town dependent, on the whole, on visitors who came in the summer to sail round the islands with David MacBrayne's steamers and others arriving on their steam yachts for the Highland Games, the changes were dramatic.

The Royal Navy requisitioned the Railway and South Piers, Dungallon House became the headquarters for R.A.F. Coastal Command in the area.

Most of the hotels and boarding houses in the centre of town and along the Esplanade were taken over as quarters for the thousands of servicemen and women who poured into the town.

There were postings to Oban of men, and women, from Canada, Australia, New Zealand, Holland, Norway, Denmark, and innumerable other countries in addition to our own people. They came as crews of the Naval vessels - M.T.B.'s, Minesweepers, Corvettes, Submarines, Landing Craft etc. Men who worked the dry dock at Dunstaffnage and the Marines who were stationed there. The soldiers and sailors (Maritime Artillery and D.E.M.S.) who joined the Merchant Fleet to man the small guns which were the only defence against torpedo bombers and submarines and those who defended the convoys from gunsites at Lochnell. The boatbuilders who repaired the small ships at Gallanach boatyard. The engineers servicing the flying boats at Ardentrive and Ganavan and those who flew them. Those who served in the various branches of the Forces, Merchant Navy, and the myriad of services required to conduct a war.

In addition there were the organisations such as the Home Guard, Observer Corps, Red Cross, Women's Voluntary Services, Air Raid Precautions and Emergency Relief Organisation etc. To these Obanites gave their dedicated services for as long as required.

All have a bond with their comrades which the passing of the years has strengthened. Many return to Oban and express their gratitude for the hospitality they found when based here and the happiness it brought them in those drab and troubled days. For what they went through, and survived, gave them a deep appreciation of the things that really matter in life - family and friends.

At one stage of the conflict there were fifteen million men under arms because of the expansionist programmes of the Germans and Japanese. Many British servicemen returned to their ship or regiment after a short leave and did not see their homes again for a very long time. One naval officer, through changes of ship in various commands, did not have any leave for three years and others worked on through the war without any holidays at all.

Many small boats worked out of Oban at that time. There were the water boats *J Hannay Thomson* and *Tonneau* to replenish the tanks of the convoy ships and warships. The Belgian boat *Berthaline*, stationed at the South Pier, took barrage balloons out to the merchant ships and these were flown when there was a threat of enemy planes in the vicinity to limit the bombers' approach. Captain Stokes, who was in charge of the Naval Base, used as his personal work boat the motor yacht *Caledonia* which was requisitioned from Archie MacIntyre of Fort William who remained on board as skipper for the duration.

Pilot boats working from Oban were *Lord Collingwood* and *Thalia*, the latter being holed in a collision and sank at Lismore. Donald MacQueen, a crew member at the time, was thankful to have been in hospital having his appendix taken out when the accident took place and all the crew on board were lost. The *Southern Wave* and *Southern Star* swept the approaches of the Firth of Lorne regularly for mines and especially if a convoy was due in to the anchorage. Various craft visited Oban during the six years of war including a Russian submarine chaser, a Norwegian whaling ship and a Canadian corvette which came for repairs to the dry dock at Dunstaffnage.

A boom was placed across the Sound from Kerrera to Gallanach so all ships had to come into Oban Bay by the North passage and were challenged, if not known, by the signallers in the lookout post at Little Ganavan. Naval ships replied with the code of the day.

Before the Second World War, and also the First World War, many Germans visited Oban in the guise of workers in the hotels and hikers in the countryside. The German waiters would hire rowing boats on their day off, no doubt taking soundings all round the coast. Many crossed the ferry to walk around Kerrera.

At one harvest time during the last war my aunt was working in the hayfield below the farm at Gylen Park when she heard what sounded like air being blown out of a submarine's tanks as it came to the surface and then the sound of voices in a foreign language. She was on her own at the time with no telephone at the house, and no transport. It was too late by the time a report was sent to Oban for the authorities to track down the submarine. The Commander of the German U-boat must have benefited from the reports brought back by these spies when he knew it was safe to rest in the Castle Bay on the sandy bottom while waiting for a convoy to appear.

Our family was involved from the start. In August 1938 my father had been enrolled as Administration Officer for the distribution of food and was also appointed Air Raid Warden shortly before war broke out. My mother was a member of the Emergency Relief Organisation and acted as billeting officer for the evacuees who poured into Oban after the air raids at Clydebank and other towns in the Glasgow area. In addition she worked at the British Sailors' Society canteen,

Isobel, Nancy, Curstan and Catherine Black

was on the Nursing Committee and also provided accommodation for evacuees and soldiers who manned the guns on Merchant ships.

My sisters were involved in canteen work and ambulance driving, two of them Isobel and Curstan, later joined the A.T.S. and W.A.A.F. respectively. Our house, next door to R.A.F. Headquarters, was always popular with the men in the Royal Air Force and I can remember one night when we had the complete crew of a Catalina flying boat visiting us. There always seemed to be extra mouths at suppertime and my eldest sister Catherine and I stopped having sugar in our tea so that there would be enough for home baking. Playing card games such as poker and sevens were our favourite pastimes but my mother would not allow playing for money so matches, which were scarce, were used instead. On one occasion, when we had a houseful, there was an air raid after I had gone to bed. I arrived downstairs with my bed clothes to bunk down behind the settee until the all clear. Another time, when I had been out to have tea with friends on the edge of town, I met a neighbour who told me to hurry home as there was an air raid warning. Running all the way back I arrived to find the rest of the family sheltering under the stairs. As Oban was considered a reasonably safe area very few people had air raid shelters.

We were lucky in Oban. There were two raids on the convoy ships when the *Breda* and the *Tuva* were sunk. Some of the raiders then went north to bomb the aluminium factory at Kinlochleven but were unable to pinpoint their target. Otherwise, when the air raid siren sounded its stomach sinking reverbrations, we were left unscathed.

The *Tuva* later had an unexploded bomb removed through a hole in her side. A wire was attached to a ring on its nose then led through large blocks ashore and back to the ship's winch, which pulled it out. A patch was put over the hole and sealed with tallow. The *Tuva* sailed again.

Early in the war friends, a mother and daughter, both badly injured, arrived to recuperate with us from the devastation in Portsmouth when their home was blown up and two lovely girls in the family were killed.

At the beginning of the emergency the local Battery (volunteers in the Territorials) were called to the colours and we schoolchildren watched them loading on to the train at the old Railway station. There was standing room only for the latecomers. The platform was crowded with families, friends and newly wed wives, there to say farewell to the departing soldiers. Oban had a small population of around six thousand at that time so we knew most of the men involved and their departure brought war out of our history books to become a fact of life.

Our next experience was the fitting of gas masks, for which we had to attend various centres in the town where the Wardens explained the working of the masks and advised us to carry them with us at all times. They were carried in small brown boxes slung round our shoulder with string but, after the first scare, it was not long before civilians began to leave them at home though the forces had to carry them at all times, perhaps not always containing a gas mask.

Later, arriving at the station were evacuees who had left Glasgow after the destruction of their homes, with nothing but what they wore and exhausted from lack of sleep. My father came home one night with a family he had found at the Police Station with nowhere to stay. They had been told to leave Glasgow because of the severe bombing and were on their way to relatives in Lochaline. Another time we had a mother and baby billeted with us. Despite the air raids they returned home after a week or two for, brought up in the Gorbals, the mother could not adjust to the quietness of a small town. My mother supplied the money for tickets to take them back.

Apparently half the children were not evacuated as their parents preferred to have their families with them in spite of the dangers. The criteria for billeting was five people for every four rooms. The children were evacuated from Glasgow, Clydebank, Dundee, Edinburgh and Rosyth and Oban was allocated evacuees from the first two cities.

Many stories were told by their landladies of the trials, tribulations and laughs. One told of sending her evacuees to bed and being unable to find them on checking later. They were eventually tracked down under the bed and on asking why she was told that "beds are only for deid people".

Oban quickly changed from the slow pace of the 1930's when the only excitement had been a visit to the Empire Exhibition in Glasgow and the launching of the Queen Mary from the banks of the Clyde, to which we listened on the wireless. Because of the movements of members of the British and Allied Forces around the country travel by civilians was discouraged, not that many would want to in the conditions prevailing on the trains except in extreme circumstances. Most times it was standing room only. Some were

Painting of Dunkirk by Charles Cundall 1940.

A.R.P. Wardens inspecting children's gas masks.

Imperial War Museum

Some of the pilots with "Susie" the squadron mascot,
at R.A.F. Coastal Command H.Q. at Dungallon, Oban.

Imperial War Museum

lucky to have a strong enough suitcase or kitbag to sit on in the corridor but there was not much peace in that position and you were advised in the *The Oban Times* to carry your own cup with you for any tea available at station platforms. Many stood all the way to London and the few sleepers were normally reserved for officers or those on special duties.

We could not even travel to our own islands as permits were required and one had to have a specific reason to go there if not an inhabitant. This restriction made difficulties for overseas servicemen who wanted to visit relations in these areas while on leave in this country. Movement for us was either by bicycle or on foot so, for many years, our horizons were limited. Not that it bothered us as we could not afford to travel much anyway.

Cars were either requisitioned or laid up for the war. An uncle had a Morris 12 which was put up on blocks, with the battery removed. The engine started on the first turn of the key when it was put on the road again in 1946. Only people with specific employment or exceptional circumstances were allowed to run a car and there were many regulations. All cars had to be immobilised when left without a driver and petrol was severely rationed. Driving at night was hazardous as headlamps were covered with masks which allowed only two thin slits, angled towards the ground, for light to emerge.

We children had the freedom of the roads and, when snow came in the winter, could sledge almost half a mile from near the top of Pulpit Hill to the end of Glenshellach Terrace without interruption and the more intrepid types would start at the top of Morris Hill to end up in Stevenson Street.

For blackout offences discovered by the wardens who patrolled nightly the penalty was £1. Non disclosure of the ownership of telescopes and binoculars merited a fine of £2. Cars had to be immobilised or there was a fine of 10/-. If absent from Home Guard duties without reasonable excuse a fine of £2 or twenty days in prison was imposed.

The wartime government appealed to the public to abide by regulations which were churned out by over a million civil servants. We were exhorted to "Dig for Victory"; "Go Through Your Wardrobe - Make Do and Mend"; "Don't Take The Squander Bug With You When Shopping - It Doesn't Help The War Effort"; "Like Dad - Keep Mum"; "Carrots Keep You Healthy, And Help You See In The Dark".

One campaign, which was adhered to by most of the population, issued posters urging "Don't Talk - you know so much", "Walls have Ears" and so on but, as usual, there were those who never seemed to understand that regulations applied to them. Letters were censored - perhaps not every one but enough to make people think twice about mentioning anything about the conduct of the war. However, one woman was up in court for mentioning the movement of ships in a letter to England. She was fined £5 or twenty days in prison. A shorthand typist's weekly wage at that time was around £2.

Practically every week *The Oban Times* contained instructions from the Government on how to conserve fuel by sifting cinders for the fire or not having more than five inches of water in a bath. We were told two layers of tissue paper would dim torches enough to be considered insignificant enough not to attract attention from passing German aircraft. We were not allowed more than fifteen hundredweight of coal in reserve and no food was to be hoarded. Most people were conscientious about saving as much as possible, being aware of the dreadful risks being taken by the men of the Merchant Navy, many of whom were recruited from the Highlands and Islands.

Defence regulations prohibited the use of small boats in tidal waters between 6pm and sunrise which was later relaxed so that local fishermen could help out with the food supply.

The crash of the Duke of Kent's plane while on a flight to Iceland in August 1942 was a shock to us all in Oban as the crew was well known to us. I baby sat for Wing Commander Moseley and his wife, who lodged with my aunt, and, it turned out twenty years

*Left:
Small craft which took
part in the Dunkirk
evcuation in the
Thames in London*

*Below:
Mechanics at work on
a Short Sunderland in
Ardentrive Bay, Oban.
The ladder on the huge
tailfin is removed
before taking off.*

later, the pilot of the Sunderland, Australian Frank Goyen, was connected to our family by marriage. His brother, Norman, stayed with us when he came on leave to visit his brother's grave, the bodies having being brought back to Oban for burial with full military honours. Only the tail gunner, Andy Jack, survived.

The Ministry of Food was set up to ensure a fair distribution of food to all and, on the whole, it was a successful operation. Of course, in the cities a black market existed with stolen food but, in Argyll, we had no egg rationing and there were plenty of rabbits to supplement the meat ration so we were better off than other parts of the country. It was hardest on single people on their own with a ration mid war, per week, of eight ounces of sugar; two ounces of butter; four ounces of margarine; two ounces of bacon; two ounces of lard and one egg - but not every week. Having six (some of the time) in the family our rations stretched for the many guests who arrived. My favourite meals were of stewed rabbit and salt herring, a firkin (half barrel) of them being purchased every autumn The rations which did not appeal to me were the soya sausages, dried bananas and powdered egg. The latter could turn out quite unlike a fried egg and more like leather in the hands of a poor cook, or sometimes even a good one, but we normally used it for baking.

My father had a butchers' business but this did not mean we had lots of extra meat. The ration provided to him allowed for loss in processing the meat and a good butcher could cut this down considerably, making more available for the customers. There were no customers who did not have a little extra in their rations at one time or another but there were those who wanted extra every week and refused to understand that everyone had their turn when there was a little available. We never had roast beef or fillet steak at home as this was reserved for the hotels and had, usually, a sheep's head, flank of mutton or tripe which many customers did not wish to accept as their ration. Meat rationing was not withdrawn until some years after the war. In fact the Ministry of Food were still in control of the distribution of rabbits and chickens in 1947 with dire penalties for a breach of regulations. My father, a J.P., was mortified to be fined on the occasion of having a glut of rabbits arrive with no way of disposing of them locally. He forwarded them to a butcher in Greenock to save sending them to the dump. His crime was that he sent them outwith the Argyll boundary.

In 1942 we were allocated twenty food points a month. Seamen and other categories were allowed twenty two points per week. Doing the shopping was a matter of juggling the family's taste with what was available and whether there were enough points to buy the food. Canned beans were one point. Canned peas four points; broken biscuits were one point per lb and chocolate covered four, with luxury in the shape of a tin of American turkey for Christmas which needed twenty points. I wonder how many families managed to raise the necessary for that?

Price was not as important for it was controlled by the Ministry of Food. Treacle went up from four to eight points per pound, an indication that the ship carrying our supplies had been sunk on passage but we were assured that onions would not be rationed that year.

Before the war there were over two hundred types of biscuit on the market but by 1942 this had been reduced to just twenty. We did not starve though many were hungry at times and we were never reduced to drinking coffee, as inflicted on the Norwegian people by the Germans, which consisted of sawdust dyed brown with a little vanilla added. After three years of war, although consumption of imports had gone down forty five per cent, there was only two months'supply of food in Great Britain.

My mother's cousin in New Zealand spent a large amount of money sending food parcels to all her relations in Scotland. When one of these arrived my mother would keep the parcel until we arrived home to share the excitement of unpacking the box. The contents varied but there would be, perhaps, a tin of butter, jelly crystals in sugary cones, tinned fruit, tinned meat, dried fruit, biscuits and chocolate. There was also one item which my mother said she would never have believed before the war that she would ever be thankful to see - a tin of dripping!

Clothing was also scarce. For adults, sixty clothing coupons had to last for fourteen months and children had twenty extra. Chiffon hose took two coupons. Pyjamas eight. Tartan skirt six. Men's boots seven points. Boy's pullover five. Overalls seven. Ladies wellingtons were 17/6d with two coupons but a permit was required and instructions were given on how to care for them. They were practically unobtainable being reserved for the forces. It was an offence to throw away any rubber and, at one time, men's socks were decreed to be made five inches shorter than normal.

We spent a lot of time collecting and drying spaghnum moss for delivery at Red Cross Headquarters as it was supposed to be sterile enough for padding wounds and had been widely used in the first world war. At other times there were appeals for medicinal plants, nettles, rose hips (for vitamin C) also chestnuts and acorns for pig feed. Anything which would save shipping space and, I presume, money for the war effort was given much support by Girl Guides, Boy Scouts and other organisations though we could not compete with the gentleman from Onich who collected over one thousand bags of moss by himself.

For ourselves, we collected blaeberries and brambles from which my mother made jam and puree and, in the autumn, we had an expedition to the woods around Oban for hazel nuts for Christmas. Any source of extra food was investigated and we thought nothing of cycling fifteen miles to walled gardens in the country to scrounge any extra fruit and vegetables they might have left.

Salvage was also collected such as name plates, door knockers, plaques, toy soldiers, candle sticks and gongs. Practically all iron fences and gates in the town were cut away in 1943 and taken to Lochgilphead where they were reputed to be still lying, unused, long after the war.

But life went on in spite of scares and rumours (strictly

forbidden). Nightschool in winter as normal, dances were held every week in the Corran and Argyllshire halls, there being a canteen at the latter. With whist drives, beetle drives, ceilidhs, lectures and many other entertainments to run or attend to raise funds for the Spitfire Fund, Red Cross, Comforts for Russia and parcels for prisoners of war etc., there was no time to be bored. For lighter entertainment the two cinemas provided films like "Tugboat Annie" and Nelson Eddy in "The Chocolate Soldier".

There were many drives to raise money for a Spitfire or a tank. A "Wings for Victory" week raised the sum of £77,408. This started with a parade and drumhead service followed by sports, boxing, rugger, variety show, Link Trainer flights and a tennis tournament.

On the Corran two Tarran huts were erected as a club for women in H.M. Forces, run by the Y.W.C.A., whose energetic staff were up early every day to bake scones and fill rolls to accompany the coffee and tea provided. I was pressed into service there in addition to working at the British Sailors' canteen in Stevenson Street. Many of the servicemen and women returning to visit Oban have mentioned the homely atmosphere and moral support provided by Helen Hindmarsh and Elsa Kerr. It was suggested Helen should have been awarded a medal for saving the girls from the misery of their unheated quarters during Oban winters. My last memory of her was a parcel received at the end of the war of a pair of silk stockings from Italy and a letter to say she had been in hospital suffering from flea bites. Visiting her in Edinburgh recently I found she had lost none of her exuberance or interest in people.

The Playhouse tearoom was one of the focal points of the town at that time for locals and travellers. It was taken over and run as an American Red Cross canteen for the services from 1943-44

The Tennis and Golf Clubs welcomed all the services and officers and men were treated alike. At the former we were ruled with a rod of iron by Miss Sinclair who made sure that no one was left without a partner and the courts were not monopolised for more

A Short Sunderland about to take off from Oban Bay.

Imperial War Museum

than the regulation half hour. The good players were also made to include beginners at times so the standard of tennis was high. The Australians and New Zealanders especially appreciated the courts which were reputed, until altered by the Council, to be the best on the West Coast of Scotland.

The addition of thousands of servicemen into the life of the town did not alter our habit of walking everywhere in the blackout at any hour. The only thing that worried us was the thought of a moment of aberration while on our way to Oban High School along Argyll Square and Soroba Road in the dark (there were no street lights) and a collision with the baffle walls which protected the entrance of the closes from blast. Many a black eye was seen in those days. One had to install in one's memory the obstructions around the town such as sandbags outside the Courthouse. Windows on many of the public buildings were crisscrossed with sticky paper to prevent injuries from flying glass

There could be times of depression when the Oban Times appeared on a Thursday with "The Roll of Honour" which so often contained the name of someone we knew but, when you are young, this does not last and the news of someone moved from the missing list to being a prisoner of war, or escaping from Germany, would lift our spirits again. Our parents must have been very worried about the future but never let us see it and we were so busy there was not much time to linger on the possibilities.

At Oban High school we had an invasion of evacuees many of whom had relations in the town. The school numbers increased by almost twenty five per cent and as male teachers who belonged to the Reserves were called up this meant an increased workload for the staff. Of course, the only time in which my name appeared on the prize list had to be the year the ceremonies were discontinued because of the war. Just fifteen, I left school in June, 1942, and started work as office girl in David MacBrayne's office on the North Pier.

There I was shown how to write up MacBrayne's books and use the telephone switchboard. Shortly after that, Archie Black, who had been attending to the loading of stores for the convoy ships which gathered in the Firth of Lorne, was called up and I took over his job. Willie Calderwood, the manager, who had married a next door neighbour of ours, gave me a free hand after my initiation into the various aspects of the work. He had enough to do with running our own ships and arranging schedules so I was left to use my own initiative when attending to the procurement of boats and loading stores.

There was also mail to be delivered to the Customs for censorship and visits to the Ministry of War Transport office in the Caledonian Hotel to collect the secret daily lists of ships in port with numbers alongside the names which were used when referring to the vessels.

At other times I might be sent to the bank to collect thousands of pounds for payment of crews and also kept track of the various vessels arriving and departing from the piers as their owners would often telephone to enquire as to their whereabouts.

In 1942 the war was at its height but one man did not expect us to lose when he advertised in the *Oban Times* that he wished to buy a castle in the Highlands or Islands, an ancient castle preferred.

By 1943 we were being warned to take care when enemy planes appeared as the Germans were dropping small anti-personnel bombs on civilians. Two American passenger ships were sunk in the North Atlantic with the loss of eight hundred and fifty passengers. There was a warning that clothing coupons might be reduced to forty two per year but, by December, we were aware that our combined forces had stayed the Axis expansion and we were hopeful that events were turning in our favour.

When 1944 came there was a positive feeling that things were happening though nothing was discussed regarding the squadron of landing craft stationed in Oban which disappeared from the bay to practice landing soldiers on Kiloran beach, Colonsay.

A friend wrote to say she had just missed being blown to pieces by a V1 Flying Bomb which landed nearby while she was helping with the harvest. The V1 and V2 rockets were the Germans final attempt to subjugate the British Isles. They could be seen coming with the long tail emitting flames and when the engine stopped anyone within hearing distance knew that within the count of three the bomb would land somewhere near or on them. A humorist in the South of England nicknamed them "Doodlebugs". It was becoming a race between the production of more of these bombs for the destruction of life in Britain and our invasion of the Continent. Again, we were lucky in Scotland to be out of their range.

When we heard of the gathering of men and materials it was unbelievable that the Germans were unaware of the proximity of the invasion. My sister, Isobel, was driving an ambulance around Southampton Water at the time and said the number of lorries was tremendous. The sides of the country roads in the South of England had been strengthened so that the lorries carrying parts for the Mulberry harbour, and convoys of tanks, could park for a night.

They were moved each day, as if on manoeuvres, to prevent any reports of a build up of forces. Any bombing raids in Hampshire would have destroyed some units, they were so thick on the ground, but no German planes flew over.

Curstan, meantime, had been stationed in Oban, working in the Meteorological Office at Dungallon for some time before the Squadron was moved to Castle Archdale in Ireland. The Sunderland seaplanes gave a display of aerobatics over the town on leaving, flying so close to the station clock it was a wonder the hands were not affected. It was some time later before it was disclosed that she had hitched a lift on one of the Sunderlands flying over to Lough Erne instead of travelling all the way by train, boat and train again. While she was billeted at home my mother was allowed 9/10d per week for full board.

The interior of a Sunderland with the side gunners ready for action.   *Imperial War Museum*

A ship with a cargo of explosives went aground in the sound of Kerrera beside the lighthouse. Mrs. Spencer was asked to go out to it in her launch and bring the crew ashore but was not too happy when she heard what was on board. She had seamen's rations but often did not have time to eat. She also remembers tinned Mexican sausages as being the best she ever tasted.

During the years from 1939 to 1945 in Oban, we each attended to our own duties but, because of the need for security, knew little of what went on around us and only in the last year have I come across some of the tragedies, and comedies, of our war.

At one stage of the hostilities a Naval Officer was showing a VIP around the watchtower overlooking the Sound of Kerrera and the anti-submarine boom stretched across it. He explained how no submarine could enter through the Sound of Kerrera to Oban Bay and that if a submarine tried to force a way through the net the lookout could press a button to explode mines underneath. In his enthusiasm he went too far and actually pressed the red button by way of explanation. We thought the war had come to us in Oban that day and Mary Binnie, walking nearby, told me the whole road shook under her. She thought her end had come. The Navy were rather embarrassed when the tale came out.

At the beginning of the war sandbags were hurriedly prepared to protect windows and doorways in towns from blast if bombs were dropped nearby. A misguided civil servant, in London, gave the order for a shipload of sand to be dispatched to the island of Tiree to fill sandbags for protection at the airfield. The Tiresdeachs were very amused, and exasperated, when the cargo arrived as it has more sand on its beaches than possibly any tourist resort in the country.

A Blue Funnel ship arrived in the UK with a full load of ground nuts and, on being unloaded, they were found to be full of mites. The ship was sent up to Loch Linnhe and, at the back of Kerrera, the complete load of peanuts was dumped over the side. No reports were heard in the town of peanuts being washed up on the shore but the fish must have had a wonderful time.

One day during the war the inhabitants of Colonsay were aware of a low flying R.A.F. plane overhead. It circled the bay at Scalasaig which was full of trawlers sheltering from a gale and the watchers realised it was in trouble and wanted to land. Eventually it came down at the edge of the bay and the pilot successfully ran it up on some flat rocks, tearing out the undercarriage. The crew tumbled out of the plane and ran off as quickly as their legs would carry them, staying at a safe distance until they realised the danger of explosion had passed.

The plane was full of bombs and ammunition. The crew explained that if it blew up there would be nothing left of Colonsay. All the able-bodied inhabitants of the island turned out to give a hand and the church was used to store the plane's cargo. The next morning at dawn it was discovered the plane had disintegrated into small pieces when the tide came in.

The coast of Britain was scoured at the time of the evacuation of Dunkirk for anything that would float and all the small boats in Oban were requisitioned. They were taken away one Saturday morning, leaving the local mariners without the means of earning a living. Mrs. Spencer was employed by the Royal Air Force for work in connection with the flying boats and, despite their protests, her *Jean* was taken away and never seen again. Another boat she managed to acquire later, from Mull, had to be documented as being under charter to the Royal Air Force or it would have gone as well. Only one boat was returned after the war, Sandy Johnstone's *Dignity.* In 1940 the Emergency Powers Act had been passed which gave the Government complete control over public property and possessions but this power was very little used.

Ian Forbes, now living in Auckland, New Zealand and one of our billeted gunners, always wore a heather coloured kilt as part of his uniform in the London Scottish though seconded to the Maritime Artillery. He wrote to me recently of a voyage he made during the war from Hull to Isafjord in Iceland on board the Danish ship *Rota*. They sailed to the Pentland Firth in convoy then proceeded alone to Iceland. It was a very eventful voyage with many attacks by enemy aircraft. It was only because it was a small ship and they had atrocious weather all the time that they returned successfully, arriving back with a full cargo of frozen cod.

Dropping of agents into France was kept secret during the war and all personnel were forbidden to mention the operations in any circumstances. One night a Lysander, the small plane designed to land in an area the size of a small football field, made a trip to an area near Paris. Successfully depositing its passenger, the plane took off again. A shot was fired, the only one, smashing their compass and radio. It was a very misty night so they could not make their way home by landmarks. The pilot remembered there was to be a northerly wind during the night and adjusted his homeward direction taking this into account.

Eventually the Lysander's fuel ran out without any glimpse of anything familiar and the pilot managed to land the plane successfully without any hurt to the crew but they did not know if they were in Denmark, Ireland or even Portugal. The pilot remained with the plane and sent his navigator to prospect the countryside to find out, if he could, where they were. Eventually the man returned with members of the local home guard. The plane had landed near Benderloch. Apparently the wind had shifted round to the South during the flight.

Taken to be interviewed by the RAF Station Commander at Oban the pilot rightly refused to give any details of their flight. As a result, they were conveyed to the cells for the rest of the night.

Their own squadron control tower had been checking if the plane had turned up at any of the RAF stations around the southern English coast and it was some time before they were informed that a mysterious Lysander had fallen into the hands of the RAF at Oban. By that time the crew were probably sleeping off their nervewracking flight and not interested in being awakened to be told they were free men.

It is interesting to come across references to ships whose skippers we knew well during the war for one would never have learned from them of the courage behind their quiet demeanour. The gunner on the *Dan-Y-Bryn* shot off part of the wing of a Heinkel in the North Sea. In 1940 she fought a six hour battle with a sub in the Caribbean and scored surface hits on a surface raider on a voyage from Vancouver. During her voyages to Russia a total of eighteen enemy aircraft were shot down and, on one occasion, she had six torpedoes running parallel to her course after making a forty five degree turn to avoid them. No wonder her Master, Hugh MacLeod, was awarded the Distinguished Service Cross.

We did not even know about the events in the lives of our own family and it is only recently that we heard some of the experiences of my brother-in-law, Roy Davis, when he was stationed in Oban as Flight Engineer, first in Sunderlands then Catalinas. I had been reading Ludovic Kennedy's book in which he relates events of the war and was interested when he mentioned that American pilots had taken part in operations with Coastal Command in Catalinas from Oban. Asking Roy about this he said that what actually happened was that the Americans delivered the seaplanes and trained Wing Commander Barratt to fly one. Then he trained all the other British pilots and the Americans were never on operations with them. Roy was Flight Engineer on most of these training flights.

When a signal was received reporting that the German battleship *Bismarck* had left her moorings and seemed to be heading through the North Sea to the Atlantic Ocean, Catalina flying boats from Oban, Plymouth and Wales were sent out to look for her.

Roy Davis was Flight Engineer on the one flying from Oban. Flight Lieutenant Hadfield was Skipper. The Skipper was not always the pilot.

The Illustrated London News sent a reporter to Oban to interview the crew after the battle as they were considered to be the first plane to sight the German battle cruiser. An article appeared with a large illustration of the *Bismarck* being shadowed by a Catalina.

My brother-in-law, having recently read the report said it was authentic and did not think anyone else could have known all the facts except the skipper.

Much manipulation of reports took place of news items handled by the Ministry of Information. The pilot shown in the article was not one of the squadron and the station shown was not Oban but this was deliberately done to confuse the enemy.

Roy was in his bunk when the *Bismarck* opened fire. He immediately rolled out, luckily for him, as a row of tracer bullets ran right along the centre of the evacuated bunk before he could rise to his feet. The pilot dived from four thousand feet to sea level without warning and my brother-in-law has only now, in 1993, been awarded a small pension for the ensuing deafness.

There was still a lot of hard fighting to be done by our boys and the length of the Roll of Honour grew. When D-Day came it felt as if a load had been lifted off our shoulders though everyone knew the job was still half done and we still could not relax if the war in the Far East was to come to an end. We did not know of the Atom bomb then and when we heard of the devastation in Hiroshima it was with a sense of relief that something, however frightening, had happened to end the relentless hostilities. It saved countless lives in the Allied armies and rescued our starving, and ill, servicemen and civilians from the death camps of the Far East, though it came too late for thousands of them.

For us, rejoicing on D-Day on the eighth of June 1945 and VJ-Day on the 15th of August 1945 at the end of hostilities, there was also horror and compassion when the full story of the prison camps in Germany and Japan appeared. We hoped that nothing like this would ever happen in the world again.

By the first of January 1946 Oban Bay was quieter than it had been for six years with only three ships in harbour to sound their sirens to bring in the New Year. I also noted that my Post Office bank book contained £92, saved in the years since starting work at 10/- per week.

Large steam yachts which had been requisitioned at the outbreak of war were slowly being released and some were laid up in Oban awaiting buyers. One, the *St Modwen*, was purchased by an Egyptian Greek and Captain Cassimatis, our old friend from the *Culebra* , came with an engineer to take her over. He invited all David MacBrayne's office staff to a party on board where Mrs. Travis, our typist, was asked to raise the Panamanian flag in a commissioning ceremony and give her the name of *Komninos*. It was rumoured the ship was later used to run Jews to Palestine.

On 26th January 1946 I wrote in my diary that Mr Munro had opened up a Chandlers shop on the North Pier and his stock included pots and pans, dishcloths and enamel basins!

DEFENCE REGULATIONS.

This is to certify that

Mrs *Black,*

of *Portlea, Oban.*

whose usual signature appears in the margin, has been duly appointed to act as a billeting officer under the Defence Regulations.

Barbara Black. [SEE BACK

Signature *Mallaughton*

See You in Three Months

On a typical, wartime, day I would arrive at the office, David MacBrayne's on the North Pier in Oban, to find Mrs Travis, our typist, removing the cover from her typewriter, ready for the day's work while Bob MacGill, who mainly dealt with convoy business, booked a priority phone call to the United States Lines in London. Willie Calderwood, our boss, came through from his room to let us know a large convoy arrived through the night and we will have a busy morning. On my way to work I had called at Naval Headquarters to collect the list, marked Top Secret in purple ink, which was used when referring to ships by number instead of their name, passing, on my way out, notices proclaiming "Walls Have Ears" and "Don't talk. You know so much".

The Ministry of War Transport controlled the ships but their owners still provided bunkers and stores and arranged for repairs and dry docking. The Shipping Federation supplied extra crew required from their "pool" of officers and men. We were agents for all the merchant ships which gathered in the Firth of Lorne before taking off, in convoy, for various parts of the world and co-ordinated with the other agencies to make sure all was ready to dispatch the ships on the due date.

The Germans announced in a broadcast in October 1939 that British Merchant ships were attacking their submarines and from then on they would not observe the International law which entailed giving a warning before opening fire. Every Merchant vessel would be regarded as a warship. At that time few, if any, British cargo and passenger vessels were equipped with guns.

The use of the convoy dated from the 14th century when an official was appointed "Wafter of the Wool Fleet" to protect the wool ships from the many privateers skulking around our shores. In the Napoleonic wars, East Indiamen gathered together to proceed in convoy for protection.

Sending ships together with escorts reduced losses considerably during the first world war so the experience gained was immediately put into operation and the first convoy, in the second world war, sailed from Halifax, Nova Scotia in September 1939. Some ships, able to travel at higher speeds than the others, were allowed to proceed on their own, in the hope that the extra turn of speed would help to outrun submarines intent on sinking them. Even one knot more than the convoy average was enough to give them permission to sail independently. During the last war, Coastal Command escorted over 6000 convoys as far on their way as was possible according to the seaplanes' fuel capacity.

My first job in the morning was to sort out the ships' mail which normally arrived in large envelopes from the owners then I hurried to bring the office ledgers up to date.

At 10 a.m. the office door opened and three captains trooped in, all British, who created momentary confusion. One requested mail for the *Empire Trader* and I obtained this for him from the mail box. Another asked to telephone his head office, Hogarths in Liverpool. After some delay, even with priority, we are connected and he went into the telephone box to take the call. We heard him ask for the Marine Superintendent and saying "Davis here". The telephone box was more useful for cutting down noise from outside than keeping the conversation private.

The third captain introduced himself as Captain Anderson of the *Ortega*, Holt Line. Mrs Travis asked if he has come across Captain Redfern, one of our favourites. "I am sorry, he will not be coming this way again". She knew not to ask any more.

The office door opened again and in came Captain Housemans of the *Belgique* with a French captain whom he introduced to the staff. He turned to me "Have you missed me?", presented an orange with an extravagant bow, then moved to Mrs Travis and, with exaggerated deference, also presented her with a lovely golden orange. There were profuse thanks from us as they were very welcome for, during five or six years of wartime rationing, I did not see more than half a dozen oranges in total. Any shipped into Britain were reserved for young children. Later, the juice only was being brought in to save space on the ships.

The captains presented lists from their chief stewards of stores to be ordered and Bob MacGill spent some time on the telephone to the butcher and greengrocer. The suppliers were not always able to furnish the goods specified but tried to give alternatives if at all possible. The stores were to be delivered to the North Pier at 2.30pm when, luckily, the tide would be at a reasonable level for loading.

It was not always possible to arrange for them to coincide which could mean a lot of physical hard work for me and Old Joe, my usual henchman, when we were shorthanded, which was most of the time. The other dockers were reserved for the loading of

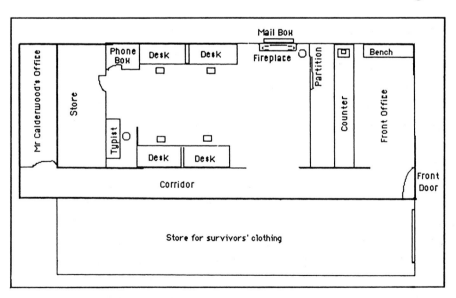

MacBrayne's Office, North Pier, Oban 1939-1945

MacBrayne's mail steamers, which were keeping the islands of Mull, Coll and Tiree as well as the outer isles, stocked with food, stock, hay and the myriad of other articles needed to keep the communities alive. Many of our ships were still steam driven so they also had to be loaded with coal. I suppose that Joe, because of his advanced age, was given what was thought to be the easiest job.

The skipper and purser of the MacBrayne's vessel *Lochinvar* arrived for mail and a conference with Willie Calderwood. They had their own problems, carrying naval personnel over to Tobermory, taking supplies to the various stops along the route, many of which had no pier at that time and passengers, groceries, calves, hay etc. were dropped into the waiting small boats for passage ashore. On other occasions they had to carry back to the mainland the bodies of crews who had not survived the destruction of their ships or seaplanes. MacBrayne's work had to be carried on all the time with customers telephoning for the price of a ton of hay to Barra or booking a bull for delivery to Salen. Where is the cattle box? In many places the animals were dropped over the side to make their own way to shore.

I wore my old kilt, as usual, not having much else in my wartime wardrobe and suffered much teasing from the English and foreign skippers in consequence. After a spate of very wet days, during a quiet period at lunch time, I decided to have a rake round the old lost property in the attic which had recently come to our attention, coming down, triumphant, with an old rubber raincoat and large, black umbrella which were put to use despite their dilapidated look. A change from being soaked in my old school raincoat while loading stores on the wet and windy pier.

We were told on the previous Saturday that ships' survivors were arriving on Sunday morning at 10am and volunteers were wanted to issue clothing and travel vouchers. I agreed to help and opened the store early to sort out sizes and allocate the suits, shirts, shoes and socks required to the men, some of whom were wrapped in

A Catalina with some of the crew looking out of the open "Blister" gun turret.

Coastal Command's first U-Boat kill of 1944.
The German crew scrambling out of the conning tower of U-426

little but blankets from the Naval ship which had picked them up.

They were still dazed and unable to grasp they were now safely ashore, clutching the travel documents which were their passport to a saner world. All the issues were documented and the paperwork had to be dispatched to the relevant offices.

Captain Housemans, who had managed to elicit from Mrs Travis that my birthday would take place in a few days, then produced a two pound bag of icing sugar, butter and flour and extracted a promise to supply him with a large piece of the cake.

Captain Cassimatis arrived, bringing out a small poke of boiled sweets for us. They may be a favourite of the Greeks but the aniseed flavour was too much for us and no one was enthusiastic to take them home so, in spite of our craving for sweet things, after he has gone they were discreetly disposed of in the wastepaper basket. His Scots wife lived in Glasgow but he could not leave his ship and it was not the done thing for skippers to bring their wives to Oban, even for a day. They were not supposed to know their husbands' route but all had their private code for communication.

The outward mail brought in by the captains would pile up so, after tying the letters together with string, I would walk to the Customs House in the Distillery where they were left for censoring. At the same time we would make arrangements for the delivery of bond (spirits) for the ships in convoy. Then back to the office which suddenly emptied again as all the captains took off for the skippers conference at Naval Headquarters in the Station Hotel. We heaved a sigh of relief for the peace and quiet, interrupted now and then by our own staff or radio officers and firemen etc, arriving to join ship and calling at our office for orders.

After the conference another influx of skippers, who had not needed stores, wished to speak to their owners. The telephones were in constant use - Hogarth Line -"Hungry Hogarth" to the crews, Denholms, Ben Line, Blue Funnel, Ellerman Line and, of course the United States Lines and the Consuls for the other nationalities,

Naval Headquarters, piers, suppliers, engineers and pubs (to track down crew). On one occasion I was dispatched to comb the inns of the neighbourhood for a captain who had omitted to telephone his owners first and they were anything but polite at his lapse.

As things quietened off the captain and purser of our ship *Lochearn* arrived in the office. "Any chance, Nancy, of relieving me on Thursday afternoon on an extra trip with cattle to Tiree?", asked Ian Macfarlane, the purser. They had been having a very busy time on the outer isles run lately and Ian was exhausted. After consultation with Mr Calderwood the take over was arranged. I was pleased with the prospect of having a sea trip for anyone proceeding out of Oban westwards had to have a permit and reason to travel.

A major tragedy! The French captain has gone off with my precious fountain pen. I was almost in tears as it would be difficult, if not impossible, to replace. The only alternative was the office pens which scratched at the paper and emitted blobs of ink, making it almost impossible to keep the ledgers unblemished.

Many of the ships sailed on a regular route to Takoradi and Lagos in West Africa and the round trip from Oban normally took three months. When the skippers left the office on their last day ashore we would speed them on their way with "See you in three months" even though we knew there were some we might not see for two years and many who never returned.

Walking along the road to work in David MacBrayne's office on the North Pier in Oban on the 31st of May 1944, I looked out past Maiden Island to see ships from the convoy anchorage moving slowly down the Firth of Lorne. It had come at last! The day we had all been waiting for and we knew there would soon be landings in the North of Europe to liberate our allies. We did not know where or when but our hearts were thankful that we were now in a position to strike back after the years of frustration and defeat.

Later, on learning of the concept of the landings and the secrecy required to make them one could only wonder how it could have been put together without the Germans realising an invasion was imminent. Winston Churchill was shown the first experimental model of the Mulberry Harbour in the bathroom of his stateroom, on board a liner, while sailing to a conference in Canada.

Every component of the D-Day armada was given a code name. Corncob was the code name for the fitting out and sailing of blockships. Mulberry for the harbours; a Gooseberry was the shelter provided by sinking a line of blockships in two and a half fathoms, or less; Whales (piers), Phoenix (Caissons), Beetles etc. Inside the shelter were floating docks, moorings for the assembled floating cranes, landing craft and barges, piers and floating roadways. It was the largest assembly of mixed craft ever seen. Ten thousand officers and men involved with over one hundred and fifty tugs to help usher each component to its allotted spot.

We had all been working to this end and the few ships remaining at anchor seemed to be set apart from the most important convoy of all - the blockships, rusting ships, which normally would have reached the breakers yard years before. Older than most of their

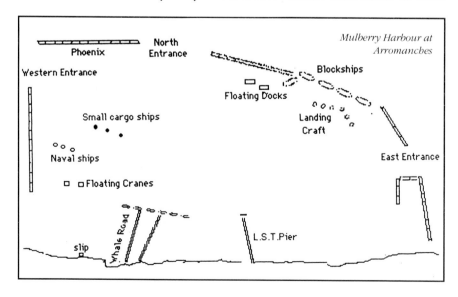

crews, they were now to be in the forefront of the action of the landings in France Ships in the British Mulberry were of Greek, Dutch, Norwegian, Belgian, Free French and Polish origin in addition to those of British owners. Many of them had been badly damaged in conflict with the enemy and one cruiser still had a hole right through its bow. The crews, who were all volunteers, were not allowed ashore while the ships were anchored along the Firth of Lorn. The ships had been stripped inside of any valuable materials then loaded with ballast and explosive charges fitted on either side of the holds, below the waterline.

On D-Day, the glorious sixth of June, the landings started and between D+4 and D+8 over 1000 tons of stores put ashore with the Mulberry harbour of blockships giving protection from the weather. Without this shield the backup for our armies could have been disastrously delayed. We owe the planners and executors of this, the largest movement of armies, navies and materials ever known, a debt which can never be repaid.

Having worked with them for four hard years I believe there were few finer men than the masters and men of our wartime British Merchant Service. They went to sea knowing the dangers.

One Merchant Navy captain had his ship torpedoed six times and a steward survived ten sinkings. Would these men have given so much if they could see the present day when what was done for our survival during the war, and the people involved, are denigrated by certain members of the media, making a good living out of deriding the lives of others but doing nothing positive themselves. I pity them.

Merchant ships were still being sunk , and crews lost, on the last night of the war in Europe, the Germans wanting to try out a new class of submarine which could reach twenty knots submerged though they knew they were defeated.

Before the war over one third of the world's foreign trade was carried in British ships and the revenue earned by this exceeded that of any export industry. Unfortunately the policies of our post war governments, and unions, defeated the Merchant Navy when the German U-boats retired from the fray and the number of ships and British seamen employed are now a fraction of those at sea in 1939.

In all, 2627 British and 2173 Allied ships were sunk between 1939 and 1945. Over 70,000 Royal Navy, 30,000 Merchant Navy and 6,000 Coastal Command personnel were lost at sea.

Maggie Sharp

Cabin Boy

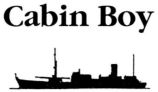

Captain McMullin, the wild Irishman, blew into the office like one of the Atlantic gales he had just experienced. "I want a call to these blasted owners of mine. The Chief Engineer is up in arms. The spares he needs did not arrive before we left Liverpool".

He placed a pile of letters on my desk to be stamped and taken to Customs for censoring. I put through a priority call and, during the fifteen or twenty minute wait, Captain McMullin was pacing up and down between the roaring fire and the typist's chair, talking non stop to everyone. And using his Irish charm to persuade us he needed to make a phone call to his wife. Strictly against regulations but who could refuse when it might be the last talk they would ever have together.

"Any mail for us?" I looked in the box above the fire, not a very safe position I now realise but it made a good excuse to have a heat at the usually roaring fire, and produced the ship's mail.

"A cabin boy is coming off the train this morning to join my ship", he uttered, after tearing open a letter "as if I did not have enough troubles. Keep him here until the four o'clock drifter" and, after speaking to his owners, he took himself off to the Convoy Masters Conference in the Station Hotel and, we knew, into the bar afterwards.

I liked Captain McMullin for he was full of vitality and though you knew his talk would normally be interspersed with oaths, like all the other visitors we had to the office, his language was modified when ladies were present.

It may have been partly cupboard love as often, after he had visited the office, I would find an orange or bar of chocolate in my desk. On one occasion a price ticket had attached itself to an

The San Demetrio safely home after a submarine attack when she was left burning and helpless but saved by the courage of her crew.

Scene at the quayside when great numbers of tanks were embarked for Russia.

orange and I remarked to our typist, Mrs Travis, "whoever would pay 6d for an orange?". There was one momentous occasion when the captain of the "Cavina" promised to bring us in a crate of fruit the following day. The convoy sailed that night.

On another occasion Captain Edmondson of the *Beecheville* borrowed a library book from my desk but I, with the previous instance in mind, chased along the street after him to get it back. The fine of 7/6d for non return of the book was a large slice of my pay if the convoy had sailed that night, unexpectedly, as had happened before.

One day, our typist was given two bananas and very generously gave me one. I shared it with the family but have it on record that "it did not taste as good as I thought it would".

I took myself off to the Ministry of Transport office at Naval Headquarters to arrange for a drifter from the boat pool to deliver the ordered stores out to the convoy, collecting the ferry books at the same time. These yellow books had a top page for the ships' chief steward giving the quantities loaded, the bottom copy was signed on receipt and the book returned to be used for the next dispatch of stores.

There were a number of books as we normally had twenty or thirty ships arrive overnight though at times there could be up to a hundred lying at anchor in the Firth of Lorn. On my way along the road to work in the morning I would look out to sea to gauge the amount of work to be done that day. I learned early to keep MacBrayne's work more than up to date, making out headings in the books beforehand, as when the skippers arrived at 10 am calls were made to owners, having to be connected by our staff as they were not allowed to make them direct. Making an ordinary telephone connection could sometimes take hours. During the war we had priority lines but even then the office would be full of masters awaiting their calls. One seemed to spend more time than most with us and he ended up marrying Agnes Forbes, our typist.

Stores were ordered and dispatched and many other matters

needed attention. There was no time for anything else but preparing the convoy for sailing.

On my arrival back at the office a young boy was sitting on the adjoining stool to mine. We shyly introduced ourselves and I found out his name was John but now I cannot remember his surname. A few minutes later he mentioned he had relations in Oban and would like to visit them if it was possible. I went in to see my boss and, as there were four hours until the drifter sailed from the slip, he could not see any objection as long as John returned in plenty of time.

He left, delighted, but still had not returned when Captain McMullin, well awash, stormed into the office around two o'clock. "Where is that young whippersnapper - why isn't he here?" With

SUPPLEMENTARY CLOTHING COUPON SHEET SC5F

Name...
(BLOCK LETTERS)

Address..
(BLOCK LETTERS)

(town)...........................(county)........................

Nat. Reg'n (Identity Card) No................./........./..........

IMPORTANT.—These coupons may not be used unless (1) the holder's name, full postal address, and National Registration (Identity Card) Number have been plainly written above IN INK, and (2) the holder's 1947-48 Clothing Book is produced with this sheet to the shop-keeper—who must cut the coupons out himself.

T51-3226

Even when you had Clothing Coupons the goods required were not always obtainable.

that, the office door opened and John walked in.

"Where were you?" the Captain asked brusquely. "Mr Calderwood gave me permission to visit relations, sir, and I still had some coupons left so called at a shop for some biscuits".

"Biscuits? Biscuits? No one has ever starved on MY ship. What do you want with biscuits!". The Captain went in to a diatribe about ungrateful crew members before realising his shore leave was passing quickly.

Captain McMullin took off again after admonishing his cabin boy not to move from the office and to divert John from his hurt pride in being subjected to such an interrogation in front of the staff I asked if this was his first trip. It was his second.

The first had been on a ship in a Russian convoy and was very cold and miserable but no mention was made of the attacks and sinkings in the convoy as we were very conscious of careless talk. Even in port at Murmansk there was no respite as the nearest German bombers were situated less than an hour's flight away.

Later, I learned that on one of these convoys forty two air attacks had been made in a few days and this would have been in addition to submarine activity. For all the ships travelling in our own waters there was also the danger of mines laid by submarines apart from that of sailing in darkened ships and navigational errors.

John's last ship had been the steamship *San Valerio,* a tanker built in 1913 for the Anglo Saxon Petroleum Company but now run by the Ministry of War Transport. I believe she was a sister ship of the *San Demetrio* whose story was so vividly presented in the film of that name.

A forty year old tanker of just over six thousand gross tonnage, more used to the oil shipping routes of the Mediterranean and the Red Seas would have little in the way of comfort for its crew in the freezing Arctic Ocean even without the hazard of meeting up with submarines and torpedo bombers intent on the ship's destruction. Extra heating pipes and insulation were installed in the ships sailing

An ammunition ship which did not survive the dangers of a Russian convoy.

Imperial War Museum

in the Russian convoys but this would not be of much help in the freezing conditions. The crews would spend much of their time, in winter, chipping ice from the masts, boats and deckhouses to prevent capsize.

A voyage in these conditions was enough to put anyone off going to sea for the rest of his life but here was John willing to join another ship which could have taken him back to the same discomfort and danger, without complaint. At his age, fourteen, it would have been so easy to opt out.

I commiserated with him in serving in a ship with such a wild Irishman in charge. We were too young to realise the responsibility carried and the fact of having a youngster of fourteen on board would weigh heavily with the Captain, especially if he had left a young family at home. We talked for well over an hour, our mutual passion for the sea giving us a basis for friendship.

We were patriots and determined to fight and win. Though young, we had read of the German's plans for the world and listened to the words of Lord Haw Haw, who broadcast local news items from Germany to demoralise the British people. This was to make us think we had many German spies in this country. We made up our minds it was not for us. My plans had been made. If the invasion came I would head for the hills with as much food as I could gather, get hold of a rifle somehow and fight to the end. I did not ask the intentions of the rest of my family! A friend, on leave from the Commandos, had shown me a few dirty tricks for emergencies, knowing full well what might be in store for us. We were living with these thoughts in our mind but nothing would divert us from giving of our best for our country. John and I were similar in our outlook.

He was a good looking, polite, well mannered boy and it was with regret that I said goodbye to him when the time came for departure.

I did not see or hear of him again. Nor Captain McMullin.

The Justifier

While I was pushing a sheep carcase down the plank on to the drifter's deck the skipper shouted up to me "When are you coming for a trip with us?" The crews of the drifters were all retired or unfit fishermen from the East coast and I had been asked a number of times but the right time never came along. It was all strictly against regulations, of course, but I knew the elderly fishermen on our drifters would see I came to no harm. They were all gentlemen.

Joining them in the converted hold after a hazardous descent on the old iron ladders we sat at a long table with the crew's bunks along the bulkheads on either side.

We regaled ourselves with black tea, scorching hot to warm us while waiting for the next load of stores for the convoy to arrive. When hostesses ask now if my tea is too strong, I smile to myself at the memory of those mugs.

I contemplated with appreciation the table set with ingredients which never varied. A couple of pounds of butter on a soup plate, a two pound jar of strawberry jam with knife handily sticking out (probably the jam was made made with turnip but still tasting good to the sugar deprived). There was also a large white loaf and jam jar of sugar.

"What about it then?" I was asked. "All right, I will see if I can get away early next Thursday, if there is not too much to be done." We were lucky to have our half day's holiday in the week.

Thank goodness for no rain today. My feet were always soaked in the exposed conditions under which I worked and, at that time, wellingtons were a thing of the future. Later I made a quiet deal with a tug skipper who hailed from Tobermory. They were two sizes too big but what of it when your feet were dry. I kept them until just a few years ago, the only souvenir of the war years apart from a tendency to sinus problems and rheumatism.

On the allotted day the Justifier left her berth alongside the Railway pier and crossed over to the North pier with the minimum of fuss as she was one of the old steam drifters. They had such beautiful lines and cut through the water so smoothly. We swiftly loaded the stores and I climbed down the iron ladder to the drifter's bulwarks.

This was an adventure - the more so as it would have been strictly forbidden if the top brass had known, though probably I had told my own boss, Willie Calderwood, as he was a very understanding type, ready to give me my head and never interfered. I had been working on the pier for two years and still did not have a pass though it was essential for everyone else. Willie was always being asked about it but I managed to go right through the War without one. It was thought I was too young to be a spy and, anyway he had known me since I was born so was not worried. All the sentries at Naval Headquarters knew me although I was given some queer looks by visiting top brass on passing through with just a "good morning".

On one occasion I walked through the barrier on our North Pier, saying "Hello" to the sentry in passing and had only progressed a few yards when a stentorian voice commanded me to stop, "Where do you think you are going?". I looked innocently at the new broom officer and said "but I work here". Another investigation was instigated about my lack of a pass.

The lines were cast off and we headed out of the bay, past Maiden Island towards the convoy. We off loaded stores at three or four ships then headed for an American ship whose skipper was expecting us and whose chief steward had asked me if I could find him a chip (woven basket) of tomatoes. Climbing the rope ladder up the ship's side was not an easy task but one of the fishermen, more used to it than I was, gallantly brought up the chip for me and silently shadowed my footsteps throughout the ship. Eventually we arrived at the officers' mess and I was invited to sit down at a table covered with a persil white linen tablecloth where I was regaled with a meal including sauerkraut, tinned fruit and **white** bread. What a feast! On leaving I was presented with a large paper carrier bag full of sugar (two months' ration for our family!) and stuffed with candy bars.

The climax of the day's outing came as we cast off from the ship. The entire crew of the drifter disappeared below decks for their meal leaving me in charge of the bridge to bring the ship into harbour. I stood contentedly at the wheel as the Justifier's bow slid through the calm water, enjoying the responsibility and anticipating the welcome awaiting at home for me and my largesse.

From a wartime diary in 1943.

CHEMICAL WARFARE NOTES
N.B.—These gases are all heavier than air.

Group.	Name.	Detection.	Effects.	First Aid Treatment.
Choking or Lung Irritants	**Phosgene (C.G.)**	Smell of Musty Hay.	Cough, burning sensation in nose and throat. Choking.	Evacuate as stretcher case. Keep warm. Hot sweet tea may be given; no alcoholic stimulants, no smoking, no artificial respiration. 24 hours rest most important.
	Chlorine	Smell of Bleaching Powder.	As above. If no symptoms after attack, no harmful effect.	
Nose Gases or Arsenical Smokes	**D.M. D.A. D.C.**	By effects.	Coughing. Sneezing. Burning sensation in nose, throat and mouth. Headache. Possibly vomiting.	Rest, fresh air, decontaminate. Wash nose and mouth with warm water. Give alcoholic stimulant. Watch for severe mental depression. Recovery in 3 hrs.
Tear Gases or Lachrymators	**C.A.P.**	Pain in eyes and copious tears.	Spasm of eyelids. Skin irritation.	Do not rub eyes. If irritation continues bathe eyes with warm water.
	K.S.K.	Smell of Pear Drops.	As above, but no skin irritation.	Evacuate only if liquid tear gas in eye. Recovery in 1-2 hours.
	B.B.C.	Smell of Fruit.	As above.	Decontamination for K.S.K. & B.B.C.
Blister Gases or Vesicants	**Mustard Gas.**	Smell of Garlic or Mustard Detectors turn red.	Irritation of eyes. Later skin blistering in from 12 to 24 hours.	**Eyes**—Irrigate eyes with warm water frequently; castor oil drops in eyes. **Skin**—Bleach Oint. Remove clothing as soon as possible. Blisters must not be pricked.
	Lewisite	Smell of Geraniums.	Irritation of eyes. Blisters appear on skin in from 1 to 3 hrs.	As above. Wash skin with soap and water. Prick blisters with sterile needle. Note.—Time a vital factor.

Survivors from H.M.S. Glowworm struggling in oil from their sinking ship.

Blockships off Lismore awaiting sailing orders on 30th May 1944.

Imperial War Museum

Courage

On a wild day during the winter of 1943 I opened the office door and rounded the partition, headed for the roaring fire after loading stores on to a drifter for the convoy in the Firth of Lorn. Some of MacBrayne's ships were still coal burners, luckily for us, and there was no more welcome sight than the piled up office fire on returning, soaked to the skin, from a few hours standing in the open on the North Pier.

Perched on a stool beside the fire was a stranger with grey hair and twinkling eyes. To me, at sixteen, he appeared to be about seventy years old. Removing my soaking coat, I tried to warm my feet in shoes wetter inside than out. I smiled, shyly, and made some remark regarding the weather. Mrs Travis, our typist, introduced him as "Captain MacLeod" of one of the "Empire" ships, which, I believe, were built in ninety days by the Americans using production techniques first introduced by Henry Ford in building his cars. Later, the time taken in building Liberty ships was brought down to two weeks in a special effort to replace the shipping sunk while bringing our supplies across the Atlantic.

While talking and drying out I glanced again at this man who had settled himself in my favourite corner. He was dressed in the fashion of most convoy Skippers in a brown suit, soft felt hat, which was now sitting on the mailbox above the fire, and an old belted raincoat thrown over the partition at his back.

I asked if he was waiting for a telephone call (although we had priority on calls it did not always mean a quick connection) but no - it was not that. Was there anything I could do for him? The captains brought us mail for censoring, ordered stores, asked for comforts for the men and we tried to help with the myriad problems which had to be solved before the next sailing.

He thanked me again and said the Skippers' conference was over, he had attended to all his business and would just sit and watch us working.

For the rest of the morning I was conscious of him sitting at the fire behind me, chatting to the others in the office or the occasional Skipper or Customs Officer who arrived on their various errands. Every time a customer came into the office, some with parcels for the Lochgilphead bus, to enquire about the departure times of steamers or, perhaps, an uncommunicative Russian lady Wireless Officer waiting to be collected, I had to open the partition door beside him. It led to the counter and, each time on the way back, we exchanged a few words.

He was a Scot, like myself and, I seem to remember, came from the Isle of Skye, although after all this time I may be wrong.

He was sitting there on my leaving for early lunch and still in the same position on my return. I asked if he had gone for a meal and was told, smilingly, not to worry about him. The rest of the staff left for their break and during the time they were absent we talked - what about I could not tell you now. I may have told him of the days we were short staffed on the pier and the foreman, Alex Clark, (a survivor from the *Altmark*, a German prison ship) instructed me on how to work the *Lochearn's* winch. Having had the experience of having three ships sunk under him, he also advised me never to leave a sinking ship until the last possible moment.

The stores were brought to the pier on a barrow then old Joe slung the carcasses of lamb, crates of cabbage, bags of potatoes etc which I then lifted, with the crane, over the ship's side and lowered on to the drifter's deck. Over the years we, luckily, did not lose any of the packages over the side.

We may have talked of the different ships and the characters

Bows almost blown off by a mine, and her deck plating buckled back like tin over her bridge, a British Fleet Minesweeper limps for home.

57

some of the Captains were - the brothers Furneaux and Captain Cassimatis, a Greek married to a Glasgow girl. I may even have mentioned my calling at Mr MacKillop, the shoemaker, with a pair of shoes for repair when my eyes were drawn to a shelf behind his head where sat, all alone, a pair of two tone blue shoes. With mounting excitement I realised they were roughly my size and asked if they were for sale. They were - and were my size! I asked him to reserve them for me and rushed home at lunch time to canvass the family for spare coupons. After fifty years I can still see clearly those shoes which relieved the pressure on my growing feet. I know the quietest hour of the day passed very quickly in his company and it was with regret that I heard the return of the office staff.

During all my tasks of the afternoon I kept meeting his friendly grin and wondered if it were always so for his crew. Most of the Captains were such mild looking men that one wondered how they kept under control the tough looking donkeymen and greasers who arrived at intervals to join ship.

When it came near time for the four o'clock drifter's departure for the convoy lying in the Firth, Captain MacLeod roused himself and, while bent over my desk, I heard him slide awkwardly from the stool and pull down his overcoat.

On turning from my work I caught sight of two objects hanging from the top of the partition, where his overcoat had been - my puzzled glance came to rest on his face, and found his eyes had lost their twinkle momentarily. Then he straightened up and smiled as if shrugging his shoulders.

As his hand reached out I turned my face to my desk, every nerve stretched as I heard him say his farewells to my colleagues and then he was beside me - he looked at me, his eyes lit up once more - "Goodbye - and thank you." My face ached with a smile as I repeated some of our usual parting words to the Captains "see you next trip". He turned, and I listened with hands clenched and beating silently on my desk as his feet slowly scraped across the linoleum to the door. His hands fumbled with the door handle for what seemed aeons of time. I half rose on my stool. Then the door opened and after a long, agonising, moment it carefully closed behind him.

I thought of the walk over to the drifter, the slippery steps, the rope ladder hanging down the towering ship's side, the almost vertical stairway to the bridge - but how did he manage? What if a torpedo came his way?

Many years have passed since that day but I can still see him standing beside my desk, a walking stick in each hand, making his painful, arthritic, legs carry him away, back to the sea he must have left years before, thinking never to return.

He never came again, and I did not ask for news of him, but the memory of his courage is with me always.

My Captain MacLeod.

In the years when our country was in mortal danger

<u>An Obanite</u>

who served 30th May 1940 - 31st December 1944 gave generously of his time and powers to make himself ready for her defence by force of arms and with his life if need be

THE   HOME   GUARD

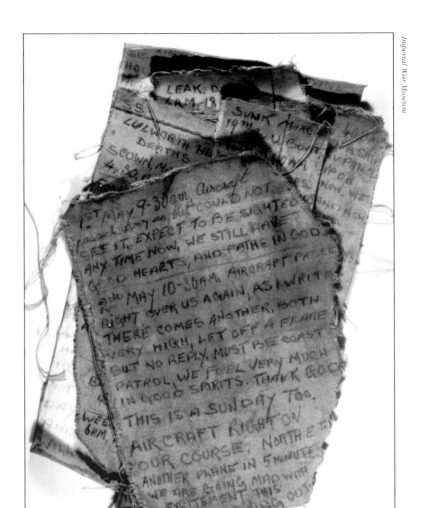

Diary written on a piece of sailcloth during their 50 days on a raft by Ship's carpenter Kenneth Cooke of Bridlington who was rescued with A.B. Colin Armitage of Melton, Yorkshire by H.M. Destroyer Rapid in the South Atlantic. Sixteen men left the ship but the others died one by one. Cooke's day to day diary described their terrible ordeal.

"Now 40 days at sea, not a seen a thing but water and water, looking for a ship or plane any day now. We must be near land, many birds seen around us. The past week has brought many sharks to us, 6 to 8 any time you look. Still two of us left but we're getting very weak, can't stand up. We will stick it to the end".

41st day "Good news today. About 10.30 this morning 2 aircraft a few minutes apart flew right dead over us but very high. We let off two distress smoke floats, very good too, but sorry to say nothing in reply from aircraft".

50th day "The greatest day of all my life, and the day I shall never forget. We were rescued this grand day by H.M.S. Rapid. To Our Lord we can only say Thank You".

When the Rapid went alongside the men were so weak they had to be carried aboard.

Florian

On the glorious sixth of June 1992, anniversary of D-Day, we were flying over sunlit Scotland on our way to the Faroes, passing over Loch Ewe, gathering place for our merchant ships during the war. My companion was Mrs Susan Emmons whose determination to visit the position where her father's ship was torpedoed on 19th January 1941 had led to us making this expedition. Susan came to Oban three years before with Dr Margaret Mann, whose father was Captain of the Ellerman Line *Florian* which had sailed out from Oban. Thomas Likeman, Susan's father, was third mate on the ship. Trying to find someone who could give them information, they were directed to me as I had worked with the convoy agents, David MacBrayne Ltd., for four years during the war.

Captain Laurance Mann was born in Cunningsburgh, Shetland, in 1885, one of a large family. He left, at fourteen, to join the Merchant Navy as an A.B. and, eventually, saved enough money to study at the Leith Nautical College for his tickets. He served throughout the first World War in the Merchant Navy and R.N.V.R., also being wounded on the Somme. Joining the Ellerman Line in 1919 he stayed with them until his loss at sea.

Captain Mann took command of the *Florian* on 11th April, 1940. She was built for the Mediterranean fruit trade, one of six Malvernian class ships, four of which were sunk during the war, but after only one trip to the sun she was sent three times across the Atlantic, the last voyage almost leading to her loss. During the worst winter of the war she was crossing the Northern Atlantic with an open bridge, only canvas dodgers shielding the officer of the watch and helmsman from the elements. The ship was badly damaged in the storms encountered and upper works and rigging became covered in thick ice. The crew had to chip at it constantly to prevent capsize.

Above:
Wintry weather conditions experienced by the cruiser H.M.S. Belfast *during her patrols in Northern waters.*

Left:
Safe ocean flights depended on the R.A.F. meteorologists. This W.A.A.F. is about to release a weather balloon.

The exigencies of war allowed only a fortnight in dry dock at Hull. The Battle of the Atlantic was at its peak and merchant ships had to be turned round as quickly as possible so the *Florian* was dispatched from Hull, via Methil, to Oban. At the convoy conference Captain Mann was told that as his ship could make up to thirteen and a half knots as against the convoy speed of thirteen knots, he could make his own way to New York.

With submarines working in the Atlantic Captain Mann decided to take the Northern route, as before, hoping the bad weather would give him cover. Nothing more was heard of the ship after her departure from Oban and on 26th March 1941 she was registered as lost, presumably by submarine action. There were no survivors from the crew of forty eight. This was all the information given out by the Admiralty to the relatives of the ship's crew.

But Susan Emmons wanted to know more. Through a friend, she contacted Lord Lewin, Admiral of the Fleet, who suggested sources of information such as the Guildhall Library and the General Registry of Ships at Cardiff. With secret records only now being released, it was discovered that the Admiralty trawler, *Northern Foam*, had reported that while patrolling at 61°14'N and 12°5'W on 20th January, 1940, wreckage was found and also a damaged lifeboat marked *Florian*.

The final link was the log of a German U-boat reporting the sinking of a similar ship on 20th January 1941 in the approximate position of the *Florian*. There were no other British merchant ships in the area at that time.

U-94, under the command of Kapitan-Leutnant Kuppisch was on patrol 250 miles North West of the Hebrides when a ship was sighted. The U-boat followed her through heavy snowstorms for eight hours until in a position to fire torpedoes which hit amidships "a ship approximately 2500 tons, speed thirteen knots, on course for Iceland".

Her log records "Loud explosion followed by reverberating blast. Stern went under immediately. Ship sunk vertically over stern". The

Florian's position was 61°20N 12°2W and she sank in forty two seconds.

Susan had tried for three years to find some way of visiting the position at which the *Florian* sank. She met with indifference from various authorities, apart from the Station Commander at RAF Kinloss who had offered to have a wreath dropped by one of their patrols.

Eventually, it was suggested that she write to Mr Johan Mortensen, Honorary British Consul in the Faroe Islands. A reply was received immediately saying that they would be pleased to take her out to sea in one of their Fishery Protection vessels. Unfortunately, Dr Margaret Mann and surviving relatives of the crew of *Florian* were unable to accept the invitation and I was very pleased to be asked to accompany Susan as I had my own tribute to pay to the men of the Merchant Navy.

After what seemed a very short flight, Mr Mortensen met us and we had a very interesting drive to Thörshaven,the capital, over quiet and well planned roads. The Faroese, treeless, scenery is striking with high hills, deep fjords, colourful villages nestling above their well constructed harbours and spectacular cliffs covered with nesting birds.

The Faroese Fishery Protection vessel *Olavür Halgi* was waiting at the dock for us at 8am with Captain Abrahamsen and his crew welcoming us aboard. Until then we had not realised it was to be a fourteen hour trip each way. We were shown to the sick bay which was to be our cabin for the voyage. Our hosts could not have been kinder and the cook could scarcely have been bettered but I was also impressed by the unobtrusive discipline of the crew whose attention to their duties was foremost.

We passed through Nolso Fjord and near the powerful cliffs of Hesto and Vaago on our way over the Atlantic swell to the lonely spot 165 miles away. At 9.03pm the engines were stopped, the ship lay idle on a pewter sea with a misty yellow sun laying a path

W.A.A.F.S. weighing out rations for the flying boat crews.

The SS Parkhaven, *a Dutch vessel which was one of the blockships used in the Mulberry harbour.*

towards us. The crew mustered, in their uniforms, and a simple,emotive,service was conducted, ending with the laying of a wreath. The ensign was lowered to half mast and a minute's silence observed, not only in remembrance of the men of the British and Allied Merchant Navies but also of over 300 Faroese seamen who lost their lives in supplying our islands with fish all during the war.

We were left on deck for a while with our thoughts, then an invitation arrived to come to the mess deck where the crew had gathered and we were given coffee and a piece of delicious cream cake before the engines were started up again.

Only a seafaring race could have understood the longing to visit a lonely North Atlantic grave by the small daughter who received a letter from her father a few days before his ship sailed on 18th January 1941 ending "When the war is over you will be able to come on the ship with me and count the fishes in the sea".

We saw in the small villages of the Faroe islands so many statues of grieving families staring out over the Atlantic Ocean.

Forces air letter sent by Bill Whyte, Oban.

Glossary

A.B.	Able Bodied Seaman
A.T.S.	Auxiliary Territorial Service
D.E.M.S.	Defensively Equipped Merchant Ship
D.S.C.	Distinguished Service Cross
L.S.T.	Landing Ship Tank
M.O.W.T.	Ministry of War Transport
M.T.B.	Motor Torpedo Boat
R.A.F.	Royal Air Force
U-BOAT	Undersea Boat
V.I.P.	Very Important Person
W.A.A.F.	Womens Auxiliary Air Force
W.R.A.C.	Womens Royal Army Corps
W.R.N.S.	Women Royal Naval Service
Y.W.C.A.	Young Womens Christian Association
Axis	Germany, Italy and Japan
Allies	Great Britain, Canada, Australia, New Zealand with British Colonies, Dependencies, Free Governments of invaded Countries, U.S.A. and others
Drifter	Steam fishing boat around 86 feet in length
Dripping	Fat for frying
Link Trainer	For training pilots on the ground
Spitfire	Fighter plane
Wireless	Radio